THE THIN WALL

Ed Ochester, Editor

THE THIN WALL

MARTHA RHODES

UNIVERSITY OF PITTSBURGH PRESS

Published by the University of Pittsburgh Press, Pittsburgh, Pa., 15260
Manufactured in the United States of America
Printed on acid-free paper
10 9 8 7 6 5 4 3 2 1

ISBN 13: 978-0-8229-6453-7
ISBN 10: 0-8229-6453-8

Cover art: Photo by João Lavinha, licensed under CC BY 2.0.
Cover design by Melissa Dias-Mandoly

This book is dedicated to Joan Aleshire, Sally Ball, Daniel Tobin, and Ellen Bryant Voigt in appreciation of their steadfast kindness, support, and creativity.

CONTENTS

(Yard Fire)

(Looking Down)

One wakes to another door.
There's the sudden roll of a chair,
compression of leather, and that smell—
bullets through one's heart—
The sky is the sky your feet are climbing to,
recalled from before. Then one sits up.
It's Market Day Along the Hudson:
arugula, quail, and wildflowers for one's love,
the one for whom, quite always, reliably,
that rose is just that rose.

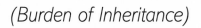

(Burden of Inheritance)

There are apples,
buckets of
and heads wet from the dunking.
A witch 'round every corner.
Ladders.
Jury and judge.
A pond of bodies bobbing, condemned.
And nineteen nooses wait.
That seven-gabled house.
Girls run the streets accusing
the accused. In Salem Village,
Goody Proctor bears her child in jail.
Our party pays to tour the next grey house.

Rose, the mother,
as her child rose,
up into the trees,
with her shattered child.

In her arms, the bifurcated child.
"Don't go, don't go," cries
of the husband. "Don't
leave me. I can't bear it,"

though surely he could
come if he wanted,
she thought, he could
will himself up, up, to join

them, his small family.
John! But there he stands,
smaller and smaller. "Look
darling child, there's your father.

Now shut your eyes and forget him."

Boys, girls, some of them siblings,
spawning in bathtubs all over town.
Drown them?
We stop short, though
let the water run frigid,
our blue hands at their blue backs.

Willed to us by parents who jumped
from the cliffs of their miseries.
Now look at their offspring. *Uphill* deposited
onto our front porches. All over town,
in the shadows of the twin stacks,
we raise them, boiling up water stews,
water broths, water purees. They flourish
and appreciate. What can we do so they'll hate us
and leave?

Both of us under one boy or another.
That's how we spent our senior year,
Beacon Hill, Harvard Square,
Coolidge Corner, anywhere
but Belmont, or Westwood Center.
Boylston Street for bongs—*Reefer
Madness*, incense, Yardley's makeovers,
buffalo leather toe sandals—her baby was born
with encephalocele. While I held her,
I hoped she'd die, though tried to love her,
four months, she didn't grow—Lucy rocking her,
cooing, passers-by smiled at the handsome mother,
then frowned—small gasps—when they looked closer.
My father paid for the funeral I don't remember.
(There may not have been one.) Lucy had others—
a daughter, next a son, then nine years later,
she drowned in Maine, swallowed by the family pond,
at barely thirty, while I'm nearing sixty, and complain.

Even from their graves their disdain
toward us reaches. Our lungs burn

from the ashes of their profits.
And now they fall, one by one, onto the pavements

they drop. We, who dig their graves,
clean the bottoms of their children,

flush out their ears, watch our own young
perish. Even dead, through their children,

they take all we have. And we give it to them
for what more do we want of this life anyway?

———

The children were left right there, weren't
moving and wouldn't—2nd pair

to arrive on our porch since Monday,
dropped off by the mayor and his wife, any

house chosen they could clamber up without losing
a limb. Barely bundled the babies were, and grey.

And frozen like kittens in March.

Worry worry worry   and pluck my eyebrows bare
The burden of all   these   children will leave me with no hair

Worry worry worry   I've got no cents to spare
Get all the kids out   out out out this house has no more air

Worry worry worry   through days of stink and despair
Just look at my feet   and look at theirs all blistered red and bare

Not a chicken to boil   not an apple to pare
Worry worry worry   and pull out every hair

The twins' teacher claimed she'd never gone skating
(so she'd look like a genius her "first" time out).
She breeds dogs. Squirrel killers with ratty muzzles.
We hoped her dogs would mess with our twins.
We invited her to everything. *And bring your dogs,*
we encouraged. We'd plaster her with beers
and leave the mutts to mind the twins. But the twins,
by Visit Two, caught on. Both dogs stuffed in a drain pipe.
We knew it warn't no squirrels they were chasing
and knew who'd done it while the youngest, by 2 minutes,
stood by, licking her chops and jumping up and down.

Even the parade of turtles
moved faster than those twins.
I urged them to hurry,
with the promise of new dresses.
All I could do not to tug them so hard
I'd dislocate their shoulders.
Hit us, they'd taunt. Why didn't I?
The thought of them tied to me even more,
infirmed. How many years of this?
And then would follow their children.

The air was heavy with blood.
The boys washed off in the Merrimack.

The girls, not allowed in, backed away
from the slim beach, up toward the mills,

some pushed into the closed-off canals—
the cold moss beds of cobble stones—

where more boys menaced, and it was only June.

What brews here, you think, *is a hard green,*
gnarled and able to grab and pull me down.
Do not spill myself here, you think,
for none will pry me free.

I know your thoughts and tempt you
with a splash of pink to lure you down,
your nostrils working madly. *Darling Pink,*
you sing, *who planted you for me?*

The stirring in your head drives you to the ground.
This is not my death field, you weep.
Keep the nightstand, your fevered call.
Oh, I am a child unworthy of time.

And so you are. Thus, I continue to take
it from you, one second, then another.

(Yard Fire)

A crow at my mouth.
The bread from me

it stole. I felt
like a flour sack,

pecked, consumed,
scattered. Enough dust

to dust. You, just gone.

When I see a woman
strutting her bikini,
I strip her of it
and shove her
into the freezing
Atlantic, tied into
a canvas sack
I've weighted down.

The bikini is in my hands
and I bury it, evidence,
in a migrating dune I determine
the next hurricane that hits
the eastern shore will wash away.
A fox might dig it up before then
and run with it into the sea
and out, all day, in and out,

dropping it finally, shredded,
unrecognizable. When I see
a woman before the store mirror
admiring her own form, I remember,
in a lemon yellow room, an oval wall mirror
and a young teen girl on the floor,
naked, her legs bent and spread,
afraid to look, so shy, but looking,

peering into (imagining) her future.

The world, how greenesses
pop up. I'd forgotten. To be

found millions of years later,
mountains of bones ground down.

The tiniest with the largest.
You rise to the top

from the Great Rift
to meet me again.

The galaxy was fertile that night.
The fields glowed swollen.
I wore his suit. He my dress.
My hand up it. Our wildfires
left our parts blistered.
We slathered ourselves
with each other, returned inside to bed.
I counted out six eggs next morning.
I was sad we ate them, the possibilities therein.

He climbs the staircase of his dry throat,
opens the door and dives out and down
the spiral narrowness of air. All he leaves
behind are those he never wanted,
but this, always, he has wanted.

It is the horse in her he fears,
her eyes, large and rolling,
the yellow crunch of her molars,
and her heavy foot aimed at him.
He hears her in the stall of night
approach, the other animals scatter,

as does the dry dirt of her path,
and the pebbles at his feet
as he moves aside, as if to invite her
to enter into the event horizon itself.
He sees all her parts stretch out,
a string speeding forward yet still,

next to him, suspended in the cessation
of time, the galloping fury of her finally
arrested so that now his sleep markedly
quiets enough for the shift of his breathing
to stir her. She licks his salty spine—
he is calm, now—pats his damp mane,

Wake little horsey.

Her biscuit in her hand,
soggy, crumbling, lifted again
to her cherub mouth, her little nubby teeth
working at it—the child crying suddenly,
her cookie lost somewhere in the carriage,
the carriage jerkily wrenched back and forth
by the mother's left foot, the mother deep
in her novella who—(yes, correct, I detest the one
sitting across from me in this detestable park,
and I, now, am the Childless Woman
Who Lifts Child from Tribeca Park After
Bumping into an Old Boyfriend at Local Whole Foods
with Whom She Might Have Had a Child Had He Not Been
an Alcoholic Faulkner Scholar With Two Children Already
He Wasn't Supporting)—who doesn't even notice,
her foot still working the carriage. And soon it will be dark.

Warehouses of palaces
Warehouses of gruel
Warehouses of lost sheep
Tall columns of confusion.

Where are we now?

We are in the state of Massachusetts
In the city of Lowell at a turn of the Merrimack
Inside of a smokestack
Inside of a cyclone burning.

Inside of a cafe on 495
Without coffee and money
Without warmth or table
johnny cakes or butter.

We walk the stacks
Of the Boston Public Library
No books paperless
No folios decimals.

Where are we going to now?

In a brand new Mercury
Black with red trim
No speedometer
No gas no feet on pedals

Headed toward the North Shore
Toward Cape Ann I believe
Green fly-infested
Yes there's Canada right after Maine.

And this very moment?

Inside our cat's milk bowl
In a kitchen on the floor
Speckled linoleum in a ranch house
On acreage many azaleas.

Many peonies
Our mother on the terrace
Her gin and tonic contained in a glass
Silver sipping straw spoon.

Cherry tree branches grazing our foreheads
Many beetles on peonies
All seen clearly from this place we want to remain
Inside forever, place of Etcetera

And very busy with potholders here
Though at the same time we can't be identified
As useful— don't take it personally
You see here we can follow the sea.

Here we may be hopeful we will stop soon
We are in a real good holding pattern.

———

The moment it became
no longer important to him to cross the street
and occupy someone else's life, or to simply
withhold from buying her a chocolate because
it would please her so to see in his palm
anything selected just for her. To stand knee deep
with her again, in the ocean's excitement.
It was the instant the sweet love between them
was no longer love that he said to her, whispered
into her ear, when he was sure she was still asleep,
I'm staying, dear. I won't leave you again.
No longer love, but something.

A lake in February—
flat, grey, smooth
and the skate blade
drives itself across the surface
though the sun beats warmer
each month passing so that even
in July, August, September the surface
glistens hard with figure 8's, hopscotch grids,

criss-crosses. When people look at me
they hold their breaths, suck in.
What, what, so what? I yell.
You think your life's any better than mine?
Yes, they all answer. So I've stopped going out.
And he keeps up the skating all year long.

Husband, who is that woman there,
that lovely woman barely clothed,
that woman barely clothed I see
in the corner of our room tonight?

A lovely woman barely clothed
I see in the corner of our room tonight.
Weapons locked up. I cannot
take arms, all my strength not to.

Husband, you know her, don't you,
that woman in the corner of our room—
take arms, all my strength not to.
You know her, you do, stealing her

into our room tonight, that woman, barely
clothed, you think she's so lovely,
seated in the corner, facing us, mocking.
Weapons locked up. Take arms? About to.

You know her too, he said. Once, she was,
dammit, you.

He looks over at her body, at rest,
examines the Tuscan peach plaster walls he built,
the six generous windows of their bedroom,
its black granite floor, massive oak armoire,
and looks away, toward the French doors,
marble balcony, freshly seeded lawn,
to the sandy path, and finally the beach itself
where the wash of waves against his thighs
turns him blue, even as he dresses in his closet,
for he has left her already; he is lost at sea.

Of course they cried at leaving,
his three handsome children, the beach blue
with their shivering.
Bundled in towels, whisked away,
howling, by the mother in a rush
to get home and feed her hot,
irritable, envious—himself a child—
husband. *Why should he be excluded?*
Why must he be the one stuck at the bank
stuck stuck stuck defending himself,
denying to his wife—my God, will she ever stop?—
that he was not the one she saw walking
into the motel with a teenager on the strip,
not his car in the lot, as she sped by, kids
in the back seat, too furious and confused
to stop and get a good look, for God's sake...

Why can't he come too, any day he wants,
his body a great water park—slippery slide,
underwater arch, fountain, squirt gun. Well,
he can. Just watch him cancel the day—Go ahead
fire me, am off to the beach. Papa's gone fishing. He's off
to where the water's so cold he'll shudder at shore's edge,
even more so waist deep, and 20 minutes in, what of it
if he joins that pretty mother and her son catching waves,
Frisbee? The sheer iciness, the jaw-snapping cold—
excruciating-- exhilaration of Wingaersheek
as each swell lifts and carries him,
his ache's a scream, so joyously shrill
it drowns out everyone—
even his wife and kids, wherever they are.

Should I not have said hello,
extended my hand?

Should I have walked away?
Turned my back?

When I offered to fix
that little patch of fence

between our yards, but first
lifted her 3-year-old

to my shoulder and twirled
round and round, singing

Daisy Waisy (dammit her name
is Daisy), should I have ignored

the child tugging at my knees?
God knows I couldn't ignore my wife,

glaring out the kitchen window,
every tree and shrub on fire.

(Looking Down)

The man stood in the frost.
Without an end of it in sight.
All the other yards were summer yards.
He stood deep in the tundra.
His daughter brought him refreshment.
Daddy, drink your lemonade.
But his tongue froze to the glass.
His breath was too cold to melt
the yellow block of ice.
Go inside he wanted to yell at her—
he didn't want her to freeze and mostly
didn't want her company—
but she was wearing only a light shift
he could see through and no shoes
and was absorbed in cartwheels
and chasing her dog and its ball.
Her skin dark as amber tea, his was blue.
His fingers cracked and bloody. His nails
brittle, his breath about to shatter.
The man stood on the crackling frost. Many hours
he could stand there, the sun shining warm
on everyone and thing but him.

He scolds, she nags. Right after pancakes.
Can't you ever make the bed?
Then stubbornness at either end of the room,

the opposite walls advance towards each other.
Will you please comb your hair? Change your socks?

An entanglement that strangles the silence.
I love you— into her hair he'll whisper loud enough to tingle
her ear drum—he'll burrow his face into her hay-colored hair,

as he grabs her hips at the kitchen sink once they've both cooled down,
in ten or so minutes. Surprised, she'll drop a knife into the suds,
cut her pointing finger, turn around to rub it bloody down his cheek

to his chin, and leap to his Adam's apple, press in a little, won't she?

I do not want to finish my potato,
but feel guilty not to finish my potato.

Many died for lack of potatoes,
but I don't want it, that potato

mushed on my plate, unsalted and dry.
Oh I wish it was an orange potato,

sweet, pretty, brightly hopeful—
but this one's white, or really yellow.

I've asked Mother, why, always potatoes—
can't we sometimes have rice or turnips?

You know how your father loves his potatoes.
(But he's gone, Mother, gone. He's been gone for months.)

He'll be back. And he'll smell the potatoes
as he comes through that door, so happy to return

to a plate of potatoes—just eat your potato.
Be thankful you're not starving.

I'm thankful, I am, that I'm not starving, but
I do not want this goddamn potato.

(Father's chair's empty as it will be tomorrow.)

There is nothing she can say about the window save it won't open—
which he knows, she's complained to him long enough. It's shutting the
    air out.

Months of this, she throws a paperweight at it to let the damn air in.
    Wind chimes louder,
what with the hole in the glass. "Cow bells," he calls them and turns
    over to sleep.

But for her, *Air at last.* Maybe now she can sleep, and tries. He changes
    the glass
but the window's still stuck and now, insult to insult, where are the
    chimes?

Stolen, he shrugs. *You did it,* she nags for days. *You got rid of the wind
    chimes.*
He glares at her, *No I didn't,* he glares some more. *Yes you did. No one'd
    steal them.*

You brought them to the dump. No I didn't. And gets up—*Goddamn
    cow bells*—
to go down to his wood shop. *They kept the whole county up,* mutters to
    himself.

If by following him,
I could leave him.
If by hanging him,
I could breathe life
into him. If by entering
him, I could extract from him
the bright light of Venus.
If by betraying him, I could

save him; the other day
I stole and sold his watch
because I was completely
dying for some extravagance—
and thought nothing of him
for the rest of the afternoon.

Your dog's dinner.
What you feed the chickens.

The mud at the bottom of the Charles.
I'm what washes up on the Merrimack's shore.

The ocean refuses me.
I clog your drains.

I'm everyone's former friend.
I'm his former wife.

I'm his are you kidding she's your wife? wife.
I'm secluded in a church, abandoned

by the church. I was pawned forty years ago
and remain unclaimed. I was happily foreclosed upon.

Declined admittance by the dentist.
Sewn shut by the gynecologist. Banned

from the Humane Society and every psychic in New York.
Fined by the mayor for walking the streets at any hour.

My palms are ashtrays for those left smoking in Manhattan's
public parks. My mouth's a spittoon. I am a lost town

under Quabbin Reservoir. Macy's refuses to deliver me.
Whirlpool can't wash me. I walked along a river today.

It was higher than yesterday's river. And clearer.
It received my reflection kindly.

You want to dip yourself
into the soft vanilla swirl
of that young boy's cone,
push your tongue into its center
but you are wrapped, head to toe,
every inch of you, and it is dead August
so when you enter the thick lake
you can't feel its green wetness
or taste or smell the sweet water
at all. While others slide off shoulders,
you can neither kick nor move your arms.
You lie beached, and stared at, sun spots
laser'd into your forehead multiply spontaneously
across your torso. And now you are banned—
verboten—from the lake. And next day, the lake,
the largest in the world, is drained lest some of you
escaped.

I found myself looking down
from the ceiling of an unfamiliar room,
empty but for a chair, desk, and my husband.
He was on the floor,
his eyes and mouth still open
and dark. I lowered myself, somehow
pumping the blood stalled in his veins
back into circulation; it was all effortless, his cheeks
reddened, he rose to standing, and through me
passed, no thank you, no recognition, resuming
his work as if it had never stopped.

How can anyone conjure the invisible
And yet the Invisible was arguing
with my friend by her parents'
stretch of river, where it is narrowest.
I walked down the path, towel
and picnic over my shoulder,
looking toward the clearing
where it's easiest to enter the water
and saw them—my friend
and the misty shape entangled,
pushing—I felt like a brush of dusk
upon them, the closer I came,
the darker they were. Did my friend
need my help? And then the stream
thickened, threatening to overcome me
and I climbed a high rock.
Night poured down though it was just noon,
my back sweating. I wouldn't see
my friend again until dinner. *Finally,*
where have you been? she scolded.

———

My job is to extract your soul and usher it
along to where today we find, north of north,
a strip of sand wide as wide, a branch of river,
leaf deep. Nothing surrounds or meets us here.
My pleasure—your contentment, your acceptance
of eternity, here—that I have chosen right by you.

———

I had to let him go.
I'd not heard from him in days.
There was no time to search the back trails
or the tunnels. My boxes were full, trucks
arriving to take all of us to the shores. We were no longer
wanted in the towns we'd filled. The dunes
would shelter us or not. Our children would thrive
or die. We could not speculate. Those days
I could not cry. Those days I could not anything.
Nothing could I do but lift boxes onto trucks that rolled forward.
And walk behind.

In the dunes, fox tracks, and—
sound of muffled sea? Where is it,
the sea? *Is* it the sea we hear?
Or—our own breaths carried away
from us and in the wind swirling—

We are many here, sand-coated
and ruddy. Skin-cracked and cold.
We have lost our sense of where.
We think in inches away from.
Who are you?

Nothing is the thin wall of glass (as thin as skin)
just over there. I think if I look at that woman's shoes,
coated in hardened mud—and if I calculate
the weight that this playground supports right now,
all the dirt, dogs, benches, swing sets, and if I count
from memory the freckles on my mother's arms and face—
I might forget about the one who wakes me by screeching
into my brain that Nothing grabs us all, good or bad, boy,
girl popular, un-, *you*. I also think that my ability
to become misplaced, to take a few steps away and find myself
in someone's poppy garden, or in the frozen aisle at the market,
or hovering at the ceiling of my sister's bedroom in Thomaston
looking down at her asleep—lost, upside down, turned-around-unable-
to-navigate-*lost*—so far might have . . . I believe . . . kept me
from the thin glass wall just over there—I know exactly where it is.

ACKNOWLEDGMENTS

Poems have appeared in the following publications, sometimes in different versions:

Collagist: "I found myself looking down" (as "The Resurrection"), "If by following him," (as "Turning"), "When I see a woman" (as "Plum Island"); *Cortland Review*: "Husband, who is that woman there," (as "The Lovely Woman"); *Epiphany Magazine*: "The children were left right there, weren't," "worry worry worry and pluck my eyebrows bare," "The twins' teacher claimed she'd never gone skating"; *Green Mountain Review*: "He climbs the staircase of his dry throat," (as "The Impulse," reissued by *Poetry Daily*), "The man stood in the frost." (as "The Least Fortunate Man"); *New England Review*: "Nothing is the thin wall of glass (as thin as skin)" (as "Nothing Is the Thin Wall"); *Ocean State Review*: "Of course they cried at leaving," (as "The Cancellation"); *Plume*: "A lake in February—" (as "The Surface"), "He looks over at her body, at rest," (as "Morir Soñando"), "I do not want to finish my potato" (as "Potato"); poems.org (Academy of American Poets): "The world, how greenesses" (as "The World, How,"); *Pouch*: "Her biscuit in her hand," (as "Evil Late Afternoon"); *Prairie Schooner*: "*What brews here*, you think, *is a hard green,*" (as "I Make a Terror of the Ground"), "Both of us under one boy or another." (as "I Was in the Commons Kissing, and Lucy Next to Me Kissing,

Too," reissued by *Poetry Daily*); *Provincetown Arts*: "Rose, the mother," (as "Ascension"); *Waxwing*: "How can anyone conjure the invisible" (as "Since Morning"), "It is the horse in her he fears," (as "It is the Horse"), "The air was heavy with blood." (as "First Summer Day Along the Merrimack River"), "Warehouses of palaces" (as "Orientation").